Activate Your Success

A Path 2 You Workbook Publication

Copyright © 2019 Shelly Licari

All rights reserved. No part of this publication may be reproduced, distributed, or transmitted in any form or by any means, including photocopying, recording or other electronic or mechanical methods without the prior written consent of the author, except in the case of brief quotations embodied in critical reviews, educational papers, and certain other non-commercial uses permitted by copyright law. For permission requests write to the author, addressed "Attention: Permissions", at the email address below.

ISBN: **ISBN:** 9781073410330

Imprint: Independently published

Any references to historical events, real people, or real places are uses only for informational purposes. Fictitious characters, names, and places are products of the author's imagination.

Printed by Amazon Kindle Direct Publishing in the United States of America.

First edition printing 2019.

Path 2 You

P.O. Box 1472

Van Buren, AR 72957

Introduction

Life can be an odd adventure. All those ups, downs, twists, and turns can make you feel like you are on a roller coaster developed purely for the amusement of some great cosmic joker from planet Xylos.

Don't judge me. It could totally be a place.

Things, whether large or small, are eventually going to trip us up. Every day we have the potential to fall flat on our face or to skip merrily through the holes pitting the roads of life like we are a tiny girl wearing a pink tutu who giggles at the bubbles popping out of the mouths of the weird people groaning miserably while lying pitifully on the ground.

Even as I sit down to write this, I find myself mildly incensed. What was originally the rough draft of the first two chapters of this book has just been eaten by an update of my software. I cursed myself for not saving a backup of my work, the computer for being a piece of crap, Microsoft in particular, and life in general. At length. And considerable volume. Hours of work went swirling right down the drain toward the data version of the river Lethe.

I screamed. I wailed. I stomped my way around the house yanking at my hair like some raving madwoman. There may have possibly been some gnashing of teeth.

After I finished throwing my fit, I came to the realization that sometimes life just throws us a curve ball. There are ups and downs and completely unexpected events, and if I wanted to look at myself in the mirror with any sort of self-respect, I knew that I would have to get off my whining soap box, dust off the carpet lint, and get back to work to create something even better than what I had started with the first time!

Any of you reading this have almost certainly experienced more or less the same issue. If not, then go you, you lucky bastard. Life will hit you right upside the head with the metaphorical Great Slapping Stick of Horrible Vindictive Fate, and you, hopefully also metaphorically, can throw yourself on the ground, kicking your heels into the floor and screaming like a toddler. After which you, again hopefully (my well of hope springs eternal if you haven't noticed) get up off the floor and go back to your attempt at a reasonable facsimile of an accomplished adult all the while pretending that your little nervous breakdown was simply a figment of everyone else's overactive imagination.

The mysterious 'they' are awfully good at making things up, aren't they? Those assholes.

The thing is, that while these little nervous breakdowns likely don't take up much time in the grand scheme, they do serve to distract you from what is most important.

I can hear you all asking (or maybe that's my husband giggling in the other room) "What is this most important thing, Rochelle?"

Well, I'll tell you!

The answer to what is most important in your life is whatever you deem to be the most important! Are you planning to start a business? Maybe you intend to put in for a promotion at your current place of employment and need to start proving that you can take on all your potential future responsibilities. Perhaps you want to make a change in your relationships? Heck, maybe you want to pack up all your worldly possessions and take off to Tuscany and restore one of those lovely centuries old stone homes like in the movie! You can change things, set the pace, even stay the same! The particulars are decided only by you.

This book will help you discover different ways of changing your mindset so that you are more able to focus your intent and willpower toward helping you achieve your best self. It will traverse its way through multiple strategies on setting goals and helping you to replace bad habits with ones that you decide are better for you. It will also assist you in discovering different methods of applying your new habits to your requirements and lifestyle and includes providing you with ideas on how to stay on your new track. Finally, this book will illustrate ways on how to get back on your desired trajectory for when you inevitably fall off the wagon.

Nothing is too big or too small once you have the tools to reach for your dreams. For as long as you are striving toward achieving all that you desire in your life, the distractions taking you off your path are nothing more than a hinderance to you reaching your goals. In the immortal words of internet meme "Ain't nobody got time fo' dat!"

If you do have time to pitch yourself down onto the carpet and throw fits, spend eight hours of your time whinging that not enough people have sympathy for you, or that those same people didn't give you enough of whatever it is that you wanted this week, then this book will not be for you.

If, on the other hand, you want to sincerely put in the work needed to make real changes in your life then saddle up, because it's going to be one hell of a ride!

The Goal Setting Race

When I think of setting goals, I like to pretend that somewhere somewhen there is a little miniature pony staring forlornly at the starting line of a horse race in Kentucky while he desperately wishes with all his little pony heart that he, with his tiny legs, could one day run neck and neck with the thoroughbreds.

Is this a depressing mental image? Absolutely it is, but it's also cute as hell, so I'm going to run with it. See what I did there? I know. I'm hilarious.

Now, imagine that sad little pony. What colour is he? I like to envision my pony with a white and brown spotted body. He has a beautiful white mane that is just long enough to blow gently back from his face in a perfectly Fabio-esque fashion. Give him a name and some personality. Anthropomorphise him. Give him (or her) a little quivering bottom lip, perhaps even a single perfect tear that trembles glistening on the tips of his lashes like dew in the morning sun as he yearns to be all that he is not yet capable of being.

He's a dramatic pony with spectacular sparkling dreams, damn it. Bob the Drama Pony.

Bob the Drama Pony has a dream. He has a desire that he longs for from the depths of his tiny little pony heart. He holds it close and true, and clings to it at night like it is his own personal cuddle pony. The truth is, though, that Bob is also never going to be able to race neck and neck with a full-sized galloping thoroughbred racehorse.

Sad but true, Bob.

But do not despair! Dry your sad little pony eyes, Bob! There may be hope for your wonder pony days yet! Just because there is no realistic way for Bob to be able to race against, let's face it, pretty much any other able-bodied horse (sorry, Bob) does not mean that Bob has no other option but to give up his dream and grieve for it in proper Drama Pony style.

Instead Bob simply needs to modify his vision of his goal so that it is morphed into something which he can indeed achieve, and this is where Bob's as well as our own goal setting begins.

The first and most important part of achieving your goals is of course to have them. Most of us probably have some amorphous idea floating around in the back of our otherwise occupied mind. Like Bob, we may simply think of someday being a doctor, a police officer, or an astronaut. Where we stall out in the goal making process, is that this is the point at which we stop. We dream and dream, but these dreams are never given form. They are never fleshed out and made real to us. These formless ideas just sort of waft about in the aether before they are pushed so far away by our other thoughts and the minutiae of our everyday lives that we forget that we ever wanted them to begin with. We stop before we have even begun.

Think about what you really desire. Dreams that you've forgotten that you even had. Wrap your mind around them just like Bob did. Cradle them close to you and make them feel real. In this instance try to take yourself back to your childhood. It's just like when you played 'the floor is lava'. It was hot, and there was a volcano, and you were sure that you were going to die from falling into molten stone, because every game you played was a vivid and inescapable part of your reality.

Is your dream that you have always wanted to be a fireman? Envision yourself in the uniform wearing the hat and heavy coveralls. Feel the weight of the fabric against your skin as it is pressed down by all your gear. There's a big red truck next to you filled with each piece of equipment you will need to put out fires, and behind you is the large firehouse where all your fifty favourite other firefighter pals hang out and wait for a call. Can you hear the sirens going off? It's all you and your team now. You're a strong strapping firefighter so go battle that blaze!

Does it feel real? It needs to, because within a few more steps you're going to use that vision to help you achieve your goal.

Let's go back to Bob. Bob wants to run with the big horses. He doesn't care if he wins. Hell, he doesn't even expect to. He just wants to run. Every weekend he watches the races and imagines himself running right beside them. He learns all the racing language, all the tips and techniques. He watches the angle of the riders and teaches his own body to adjust for them just as if they were seated upon his own back.

Finally, Bob feels like he is ready to meet his dream. He decks himself out in a size appropriate saddle complete with a glued-on action figure jockey, and he heads out to the racetrack. Bob has no time for the distractions going on around him. He is focussed on the goal!

Sneaking into where all the larger horses are being led, he sidles up into the last spot, taking the place of a horse whose owner had suffered some unfortunate… ahem… car trouble. Which Bob certainly had nothing to do with.

No one seems to notice that Bob or his tiny plastic jockey are even there. Bob doesn't care. He's going for it!

The starter pistol is fired, and all the horses burst from their positions. Bob runs his race to the laughter and jeering of the audience and unsurprisingly comes in dead last.

Has Bob accomplished his goal? Perhaps. There are two ways that this can be interpreted. Either we can say that Bob accomplished his goal because he was on the racetrack with the horses that he so admired, or we can say that Bob failed due to the fact that he was never truly in the running for any placement other than last.

Let's say that we agree that Bob did indeed accomplish what he set out to. He prepared the best that he could. He studied, practiced, and had the drive to work toward what was, for him, a seemingly unattainable goal. Bob made it to the track and ran his heart out. He paid no attention to the people laughing at him from the side lines, he just went out there and did his thing because that was the bit that was important to him. It wasn't the winning; it was the feeling of being part of something so much bigger than himself.

Don't believe me? I can offer you another example of the underdogs who keep soldiering on. Discounting Thermopylae and things that happen in the movies quite often (see Cool Runnings, Dodgeball, and about 7,000,000 others. They're everywhere.) let us instead examine the case of Steven Bradbury.

Steven Bradbury is a short track speed skater from Australia. He was a four-time Olympian as of the writing of this book. That seems successful enough, right? The sheer determination and skill required to qualify four freaking times in a contest with people from all over the world who have all been deemed to be the best of the best is astounding. Not to mention the wheel barrel worthy balls required by a guy from Australia who is going to compete in ice sports with guys from places like Russia and Norway. This guy, though, through sheer nerve and skill and kind of a happy accident or twenty-five won!

Granted, it may have been because all the other people ended up in a giant people pile, but that is totally not Steven's fault. He kept going, kept pushing, and kept trying. Steven Bradbury, speed skater from an entire bloody continent notorious for both heat and great expanses of not a lot of ice, beat all those other people who seemed to be better equipped for the job by simply keeping on with his keeping on. Go Steven! Also, Bob is on line 2.

The second way that we can look at Bob's, and even Steven's, run is that they failed. Both contenders may have made it to the race, but they didn't win, or at least didn't win because they were stronger and faster than the other contestants. Bob didn't even make it to the race on his own merit. He simply took the short route (Ha! I couldn't resist.) and snuck in behind the back of those who had worked hard to get where they were. Steven won because he skated his race far enough behind everyone else that he was able to avoid the pileup of all the other skaters and swerve his way to victory.

Here we have a perfect example of two completely different outlooks on the exact same scenario. Which one is correct? Both? Neither? Actually, the correct answer lies only in the way in which you yourself define your goals.

What is a win to you? You'll need to choose a position because that will be your finish line.

Just like Bob and Steven, you must know where your finish line is so that you know when you have crossed it. Lack of specific goal definition is the reason why most of us just wander blankly through our lives without accomplishing much more than the occasional extra trip to the mall. We have no clear definition of what counts as a win or loss. After all, if there is no finish line, then how will we know how much further we need to go until we've won?

Just as you built up the image of your pony earlier in this chapter, think about where you want your finish line to be. This is your setup to a concrete goal. Do you want to make it to the starting gate? Would you be happy to simply finish the race? Is your strongest desire to come in first, or at least in the top three?

It is your goal so you should choose what is important to you!

Whatever you choose is just fine. Keep this thought right in the forefront of your mind when you are setting your goals. Your goals are yours! No one can make them for you. You define them. You will fight for them, struggle toward them, and dream of them. Great or small your goals are yours. Make them; change them; completely discard them. It is your life and your choice. First, though, you need to know what you want so that you can pursue it with everything that you have. The following activity will help get you started.

Activity:

Jot down at least two goals. Be as specific as necessary. If the large goals seem too daunting, then start small. Something as simple as "I will make my bed before I leave for work" will get you started on the right path. Just be sure that you have chosen something that you can not only accomplish but will also allow you to have an observable result so that you are actually able to observe your successes.

Be sure that you put a time limit on your goal! It is ever so easy to procrastinate to the point of never achieving a thing if you don't have some sort of deadline even if it is one that you've set yourself. Especially when you are already accustomed to putting things off until approximately never.

No goal is too big or too small. Write it down:

If after a week or two of attempting to meet your new goal you have discovered that you have chosen a goal that you simply cannot stick to, then you need to re-evaluate. Are you determined enough to meet your goal? Do you need to narrow down your focus? If not, then is it too difficult or involved?

For beginners simple and easy is better. After all, the point of this exercise is for you to become accustomed to setting and accomplishing goals, not to overwhelm yourself to the point that you're hiding your eyes while huddling in the corner from the stress of it!

Any goal that you reach is a step forward. At first you may only feel that you are able to commit to making your bed in the mornings or doing the dishes each night. Perhaps you might set a specific day in which you will vacuum or finish your laundry. For those of you who already have more goal accomplishing knowhow, extend your practice to making even more new goals. If you have your day to day routine down pat, consider making longer reaching goals. Stretch out to the next week, month, or even years!

Remember

Failing to meet your daily goal does not mean that you are hopeless!

Don't quit. Just get up the next day and try again. Practice makes perfect!

Ok, I have a goal. Now what?

Firstly, you are going to have to change your mindset. After all, those routines and rote thoughts of 'this is good enough' and 'this is just how it is' are no longer serving you. You want to change your life, but you just don't know what to do. You know that you have tried to stick to your new year's resolutions before, and like so many people who had tried and failed before you, you followed them religiously for the first few days or weeks. Then, ever so slowly your commitment began to fade away. Your fire of determination burned out just as swiftly as it had ignited, and you went back to the same comfortable but slightly unhappy life that had served you in good stead for however many years before.

Don't feel bad. It is quite easy for people in general to fall into habits or routines; yes, even the more adventurous ones. As humans we tend to find a trail that is easy enough, and we follow that same route every day even if there is suddenly a new and perhaps even superior way to get from point A to point B. We just keep going the same way again and again simply because we are so comfortable in our well-worn path. What we must now resolve to do is become aware of this tendency and then actively refuse to fall into the proverbial pitfall.

Here is an excellent example: Children are not born knowing how to walk. They must struggle to learn. They begin with rocking on their hands and knees. Soon after they start to crawl, they set off to explore any areas they can access. Pudgy little knees and palms scuff over grass, carpets, or hardwood floors. Shakily, they reach upward and haul themselves upright for the very first time, then in no time at all they release the safety of their handholds and take a few awkward steps into the rest of their lives.

Of course, they'll end up eating dirt a few times. They get ahead of their current skills in their undertaking to improve their abilities. They scuff their chins and bruise their knees and diaper clad bottoms, but eventually they are running full tilt down the hall and cackling with the joy of their freedom from the confines of the things that they knew before.

This is the way of humans. We improve. We laugh maniacally in the face of the potential danger hidden by the unknown and approach the adventure of a new and uncut trail with the same enthusiasm as a baby taking its first steps. Just ask an explorer or astronaut how they feel about knowing that they are rushing headlong into dangerous and uncharted territory which may mean their death, and I think they would tell you that they would never trade the rush of excitement and adrenaline for the safety of following the well-trodden path.

Poets and philosophers have long extoled the merits of roads less travelled. Science and technology have pushed the bar of the status quo ever upward, and they have all done it by saying "Here I come world! I do not believe that this is the end! I will go beyond the line of fantasy and reality! I will be the one who does the impossible!"

Every single one of these people from the toddler to the PhD in physics have one thing in common: the refusal to stay in the comfortable hammock of the familiar. So, a new thing may make you uncomfortable. So what? Be uncomfortable! For the most part it's probably not going to kill you, though kindly do keep in mind that I don't suggest you jump out of a perfectly good airplane without a parachute just to see what happens. Situational awareness is also a thing, which I feel is a perfect opportunity to offer an example.

There is a person (whom I will not name) that I am personally acquainted with whose mind immediately jumps to the worst-case scenario for any given situation, rather like the father from Disney's The Croods whose stories always ended with a huge red handprint of death. The situation couldn't have been more wholesome and innocent at first glance, but fear consistently lead them to interpret each situation into something that leads to a swift and gruesome demise, potential exposure to an STD or twelve, and probably tentacle porn.

I am not making this up, and you know who you are.

The fact is that in your life there is always some factor of danger. The person from the previous example recognized that their fear was holding them back from experiencing all that life had to offer and they have worked hard to change their life. They set goals, made lists, followed programs, and now they are operating at a much healthier level. They have a better grasp on their life than I do on most days!

How did they make these changes stick? They changed their way of thought. Sounds relatively simple, right?

It isn't exactly as easy as it sounds, but what are you to do if changing is so hard?

Sun Tzu said in *The Art of War* that all war is deception. You must realize that you are indeed involved in a battle. You are fighting against yourself. You are attempting to subvert years of ingrained thoughts and practices. You are fighting against others in your life who may not want you to succeed, and those who at the very least may be afraid of you changing. You are locked in a life and death struggle to grasp the fullness of the life you want and to avert the death of your dreams.

So, you're going to learn to trick your brain.

You thought I was just being philosophical with that Sun Tzu reference, didn't you? No such luck, my friends! He has many interesting and applicable things to say on the topic of deception and warfare, and if you've not read the Art of War, I would suggest it as a nice bit of supplementary reading. Now though, we're going to apply some good old military grade chess approved tactics, along with some science, zen practices, and good old Machiavellian schemes to help us realise our aspirations. Sound like fun? Well, we're doing it either way, so suit up, strap in, and enjoy the ride!

The art of deceiving yourself is one at which many people excel. Unfortunately, it is a talent that most use to their own detriment in effort to maintain their familiar patterns. Those who are self-deception artists wilfully ignore that their life is in shambles, convince themselves that they are genuinely happy working a dead end job for minimum wage, and turn a deliberately blind eye to the fact that their spouse is having an affair with the secretary, the exterminator, or a neighbour two doors down. What we must do now is turn that mastery away from evil and return it to the correct side of the conflict.

Activities:

#1

Start your day with a short meditation. Settle somewhere quiet if possible and reflect on the good changes you have achieved or the ones which you are about to begin. Remind yourself that you have/are worth every good thing that you have/will gain(ed). Look at yourself in the mirror. Make eye contact. Say to yourself:

I am worth something. I deserve to work on myself. I am becoming all that I ever wanted to be!

Repeat your mantra to yourself periodically throughout the day. Stop by the mirror on the way out of the washroom or give yourself a quick pick-me-up in the rear view.

Say it until you believe it, because it is true!

Write down at least 5 good things about yourself:

#2

If you don't already, journal your thoughts and feelings about your personal journey. Take up a blog or vlog. Whatever method you choose, pick a time where you will be most likely to check in and follow through. This will allow you to have solid evidence of your progress. Sometimes it is difficult to realize just how many steps we have taken down the road to success because the scenery changes so slowly. When you do your check-ins try to list at least 5 positive things that have happened since your last journaling session. Focussing on the positive rather than the negative will not only improve your overall outlook on life but will also allow you to alchemize your perceived failures into a learning experience so that you may excel when you undertake the task next time.

Write down all your achievements no matter how large or small. Record places where you have fallen short of your goals and make a list of things that you could have done or ways you could have reacted to a situation differently.

#3

Change up your routine. Each day find something just slightly new or different to do. Run your usual jogging route from the opposite direction. Go on a flower viewing walk or spend 15 minutes outside on your porch watching the birds. Wear something new to work. Even the smallest change in your usual routine will jog your mind into a sharper awareness where it will begin cataloguing new experiences.

Your mind is now being reprogrammed! Fill it with kind thoughts and feelings of accomplishment! Be excited each time you see a new bird or beautiful bloom.

You are creating your success by becoming aware of the wonderful opportunities which exist all around you!

Write down 3 ideas on how to change up your routine:

What if I fall off the Wagon?

In 2012 there was a man by the name of Tim Wong. Have you heard his story? It's wonderful. Tim Wong is a fellow who is an aquatic biologist for the Academy of Sciences in California. His profession sounds like it should offer enough excitement and challenges, but in addition to caring for alligators, stingrays, and other aquatic animals, he also raises butterflies in his free time.

A childhood hobby developed into a lifetime of love for Tim Wong. What began with him raising Painted Lady butterflies as part of an elementary school classroom project developed into him catching wild butterflies near his home so that he could study and raise them.

Years into his lifelong fascination with butterflies, he learned about the plight of the Pipevine Swallowtail butterfly. These butterflies were becoming increasingly rarer because the single plant upon which the caterpillars feed (the California Pipeline) were less available within the city, presumably due to it being a potentially undesirable plant in area lawns.

Those little butterflies were in trouble, and Tim Wong wasn't having that!

No. He was saving those butterflies! He had his goal and set out to achieve it. After a bit of searching, he was able to locate the California Pipeline in one of the botanical gardens. Upon explanation Tim was allowed to take a few clippings of the plant. After proper propagation of the caterpillars' food source he built an enclosure large enough that the future butterflies would have the space they needed to be free and happy, and where they would be able to do butterfly things. Tim also ensured that they would have exposure to the natural outdoor environment including sunlight, airflow, and temperatures. This enclosure would keep the little darlings safe from predators as well as allowing them to have a better chance of finding the perfect partner for making new butterflies.

So, Tim Wong, hero of butterflies everywhere, biologist of aquatic animals, more or less singlehandedly restored the California Pipeline Swallowtail butterfly to the city of San Francisco with a little DIY, a little self-taught knowhow, some elbow grease, and a prayer.

This sounds great doesn't it? Of course, it does. A man being a white knight for the conservation of little helpless gorgeous creatures of love and happiness is the fodder of legend, children's stories, and every single beat of a romantic's heart. I defy any of you to be unhappy in the presence of a butterfly. Who could hate butterflies?

While this makes for a lovely story, do you think that Tim never had an off day? How many times do you think that Tim got up, went outside to check his beloved insects, and discovered that something had happened to them? There are many things that could have gone wrong. Tim could have forgotten to secure the door and they could have escaped. A predator could have gotten into the enclosure and eaten each and every one of the little lovelies. They could have developed a butterfly/caterpillar illness and then all died, and that's just what could have befallen the bugs!

I'm sure that throughout Tim's life he had days where he had a cold or the flu and had to drag himself out and into the enclosure so that he could be sure that his pets were taken care of. Mayhap he had a broken bone, or mono, or an emergency colonoscopy… well. You get the idea.

The point is that everyone has off days. Each of us has had a day where we are tired, depressed, ill, or forgetful enough that we push things off until later. This becomes a problem when the "I'll do that in an hour" becomes "I'll do that tomorrow, or next week, next month, next year…" because then nothing is achieved. We become still, stagnant, only barely coasting through life in a fog of should have, could have, and would have.

Don't fall into this trap!!!

You are 100% strong enough to handle this journey. Will you stumble sometimes? Of a certainty you will, but do not fret. There are three keys to your future success. Desire, deliberation, and determination.

In the previous chapters you have pondered over what it is that you desire to do. You have thought, struggled, and possibly even cried because you have a dream. Perhaps you wish to be free from being forced to choose between food for your children and making sure that they have clothes for the coming school year. Maybe you want to prepare for retirement or choose the right college so that you can become a great teacher. You could even want to collect ceramic unicorns.

Disney wrote a whole song about it.

The point is that you started with a dream, now you must make it a reality. You have set your goals both small and large and have hopefully completed the activities designed to show you that you are possessed of enough skill and worth to obtain them. You have learned to centre your mind on the task at hand and have changed your way of thinking so that you now understand that you are worthy of your successes and deserve to have your best life.

So, what is your next step? Do you know how to achieve your goals yet? If so, great! Some of you may have read Desire, Deliberation, and Determination and immediately known where this is going. Others of you looked at those words, immediately started thinking of Harry Potter books and allowed your mind to wander over to consider what Daniel Radcliffe might be getting up to these days.

Congratulations. You have just failed Determination.

That's ok. We'll fix you.

First, though, let us begin with Deliberation. In order to achieve your goal, you must first have one. You can use one from the list in section one or think of a new one. Next, you must believe yourself capable of reaching your personal finish line, which you worked on in Changing Your Mindset. Now, you are taking your next steps toward becoming your own personal success story. How in the world are you going to get there?

When you take a trip you obviously know where you are starting. Hopefully, you know approximately where you want to end up. What you aren't yet sure of is what route is best for you to take in order to get there.

You could, of course, just set out in the general direction of your destination and hope that you will arrive eventually, but this is not going to allow you to make your trip in a timely or logical fashion.

My grandfather was famous for doing this. Any time he would say that he was taking a 'short cut', you knew that you better grab some snacks and drinks, hope that he wasn't going off-road so that you would have a place to pee, and strap in because you were going on a six hour long adventure called "Where the hell am I?" so that you could find places that you (and he) had never been before!

If that is what you were going for, and the destination wasn't as important as the trip, then great! That is also a wonderful goal! But, if you are more interested in the destination, then you need to find your way.

You know you need to grab a map (or open Google Maps, MapQuest, etc.) find where you are right now, and then locate the place where you want to end up. Then you deliberate. You plan the best path down to the last turn. You think of where you can stop for fuel, find places to eat and to take potty breaks, and note down hotel or motel rooms within your budget.

You don't want to get lost with no bathroom or place to stay now do you?

This 'road map' is how you will reach your goals. You know where you are now. You know where you want to end up. Now all you will need to do is choose the best way for you to get there. Talk to others who have taken the same or similar journeys. Learn what pitfalls to avoid. Ask about when and where are good places to re-evaluate.

Keep track of where you have already been, and most importantly

KEEP ON THE PATH!!!!

Don't get lazy. Don't try to cheat your way through. We all try it. It never works. Don't skip steps and think that it will serve you just as well in the long run. If you find that your current path is no longer serving you, reassess and then deliberately change your direction. You can always change where you're going. Just don't try to take off and meander your way through. If you have no plan at all, and occasionally even with a solid plan you will stumble, and you will fall. Be sure that you have a plan to help you recover. Failure is simply a lesson from the universe on how to improve. Just get up and try again, but remember:

If you try to run before you can even crawl, then you are going to fail.

That is not to say that you must know everything about your adventure before you begin. Firstly, that is an impossible task. Secondly, we as humans will always continue to learn and gain experience the further we advance through life, work, relationships, etc. I simply mean that you must choose a beginning and an end to your path before you take off on your quest, even if the end is the journey itself. Know what you are working toward so that you will know when you get there! The following activities will help you discover your own way.

Activities:

#1

Grab a paper, notebook, open a computer document, or use the space below for note taking. Write your goal at the top of the page. Jot down any steps you know that you will need to take to achieve it. Don't worry about any of them being in any particular order. Just get down what you know, even if that is to research the topic further.

#2

Look at your list from Activity 1 in this section. Is there anything on there that you would need more information on? If one of the steps to meet your goal is to have a website what do you require to do this? Do you know how to build one? Need a webhost? Make subsections of your list that would assist you in reaching all your milestones on the way to your larger goal. Do this as many times as you need.

The End of the Road?

Now you know what you need to do or to have in order to accomplish your bigger goal. Great! All that's left is to go for it right? Right!!

It's not often that the perfect segue comes along, but this is it! Of course, then I had to ruin it by pointing it out. Nevertheless, it still manages to bring us smoothly and directly to determination. Are you determined to reach for everything you desire? Are you going to get up from a failure and dust off your sore knees because they've not even had time to heal from the last time you stumbled?

As I stated before, you are going to fall. This is a fact. It is going to hurt. You'll have bruised pride, a broken ego, and potentially hurt feelings before you are done.

People will attempt to hinder your success. Sometimes it will be purposeful. Someone you know and love will try to stop you because they are afraid you will fail, or because they are terrified that you will potentially succeed. Your grandmother might tell you that you are going to be murdered by a serial killing drug addict cannibal if you take off to the big city. It sounds ridiculously hilarious but mine actually said these words to me nearly verbatim before I took a trip to New York.

Occasionally it will be accidental or at least done without thought. Your best friend may tell you that you don't have what it takes to start something or that you are not good enough to finish it because they are afraid that you will forget them when you have your new life. Your mother or father could tell you all about how you have a responsibility to the family business or that a sibling, or cousin whoever, or aunt so and so will just be devastated if you move.

I've seen this in action. I have watched as a person threw away their dreams for their life, observed tearfully as every goal a person had was shattered against the feelings of obligation to the happiness and peace of mind of parents and siblings for whom they never should have been forced to take that responsibility.

It happened to my cousin. She was the only girl out of five children. We were only a month apart in age and grew up in a very close-knit family which made us the best of friends. We played together and dreamed together. Every weekend when our fathers were out hunting or fishing or whatever grown men got up to in those days, we made our plans.

We were going to travel the world. We'd start an all-girls rock band and be rich and famous. Our husbands, which we would find during or after college, would be handsome and gentlemanly but would still be able to hunt and fish and do all the things our daddies did. They would never hurt us, and we would be happy. She wanted three children, and I would be the crazy aunt type person who would not have any kids of her own but was always fun when she came to visit.

It was great! Everything would be wonderful, peachy, glorious, and we would live forever in a rose-coloured world of awesome!

Eventually, those little girl dreams grew into ones that were more suited to an adult. I still didn't want children and had decided that marriage was no longer something I wished for. She still wanted a home with a husband, dog, and two point five kids. I think there were mentions of a cute little white picket fence. We still both wanted to travel. Thoughts of the rock band fell to the wayside while we thought of what we wanted to study in college. She wanted to be a teacher. I wanted to be a writer with a degree from Harvard. We had grown and changed but were still feeling out our own ways.

When both of us turned eighteen we were ready. We had been planning this for years. The summer after high school we were taking our very first trip to the ocean. It was, for us, the start of our adventure. We couldn't have been more excited because we had never done anything like it before.

Then came the time for us to leave.

It was a beautiful day; the road was calling our names, and I was on my way to pick up my cousin when I got a phone call. She wouldn't be going. I asked her why, and I'll never forget what she said.

"Mom is crying, and she is begging me not to go. I can't make my mother cry."

That was twenty years ago, and she is still living in that same house with her mother. She's rarely had a job, has no husband who is a gentleman or otherwise and no children though she does still help her mother care for the younger sister that her mother and father adopted a few years ago. She rarely leaves her room and even less so her house. Most people that I've asked about her barely remember her.

Personally, I went on to have my ups and downs. I took that trip to the beach and beheld the glorious majesty of the ocean for the very first time. Since then I've seen two more oceans. I've had a few jobs, and I've enjoyed some more than others. I've travelled the United states from side to side and end to end. I never did get to Harvard, but I did go to college for a degree in Psychology. I ended up married to a man who drives me crazy and yet still opens the door for me even when he is mad at me. I have a beautiful daughter who is the light of my life, though her teenage attitude sincerely makes me want to rip my hair out.

I'm still not in a rock band, but I do sing karaoke when the mood strikes. I have lived my life. I'm still living it. Each day for me is a new adventure. Sometimes those adventures have consequences that I never thought about, but I have my cry, get up, and try try again.

That is my determination. The decision that I make to live every single day to the best of my ability. I want to slide into my coffin sideways yelling "Whoo! What a ride!"

I've had days in my life that were so bad I never thought I would be able to drag myself back up. You will have those days too. Days when life beats you down so hard that you just want to lie back in the pool of your bloodied emotions and say "I'm done. I can't take anymore. It's too much!"

On the good days you will think that moment will never arrive. You cannot envision a time when you will be at rock bottom and there is no place left for you to fall. It is inconceivable to you that you will want to do nothing more than huddle under a blanket and let silent tears trickle down your cheek because you are so broken that you can't make a sound and so tired that you won't be capable of lifting a hand to wipe them away.

The hardest thing to handle will be that there may not be anyone there to do it for you. Rather than helping you to your feet and saying "I know you can't keep going; let me carry you", people who were supposed to be your support and love you will titter behind their hands while whispering to their neighbour that they knew you would fail because you will never amount to anything.

Are you ready for it?

No.

We never are. We think that those closest to us would never hurt us that way. Until they do. It probably won't be everyone, but it could be, and we could never be prepared.

The question is can you pull yourself back out of the hole? Can you come back even stronger than before?

Sometimes you will have time to rest and recover. Sometimes you won't. Either way, the only way that you are going to succeed in getting up when all seems lost and the light of your previous triumph has faded is with plain old simple stubborn selfish determination.

There are no activities for this section. Only a simple yes or no question.

Do you have what it takes?

About the Author

For more than fifteen years Rochelle Renee has worked in the healthcare industry. After discovering within herself a desire to help people in a more direct capacity, she began attending university with a major in applied psychology before resolving to become a personal consultant. Using the methods that she learned through both individual experience as well as intensive study, Rochelle set forth on a journey to share her discovery of self-improvement methods with the world.

Currently, she happily resides in the beautiful Arkansas River valley with her husband and daughter, though she still has those travel plans.

www.ingramcontent.com/pod-product-compliance
Lightning Source LLC
Chambersburg PA
CBHW030737180526
45157CB00008BA/3204